In this story
short a vow

Do you remember these words?

had   can

Can you find these words and sound them out?

plan   band   glad   sad   clapped

Here are some fun My Little Pony words:

start   sang   song   sing

Here are some new sight words:

wanted   don't   be   was

Cotton Candy had a plan.
She wanted to start a band.

The ponies were glad.
They liked Cotton Candy's plan.

Sunny Daze sang.

She sang a song.

Cotton Candy was sad.
She wanted to sing a song.

"Don't be sad," said the ponies.
"All of us can sing a song."

Cotton Candy was glad.
Everyone clapped
for the band.